LIVING BY HIS WORD

MERRILL PHILLIPS

Order this book online at www.trafford.com
or email orders@trafford.com

Most Trafford titles are also available at major online book retailers.

Printed in the United States of America.

ISBN: 978-1-4907-2637-3 (sc)
ISBN: 978-1-4907-2638-0 (e)

Trafford rev.   01/29/2014

 www.trafford.com

North America & international
toll-free: 1 888 232 4444 (USA & Canada)
fax: 812 355 4082

Contents

LIVING BY HIS WORD is a collection of short articles that can make daily living a little easier and enable one to get a better understanding of man's relationship with his creator, God. God, through His Son, Jesus Christ created this earthly planet upon which we live. He set man free to live his or her life here on earth in whatever manner they choose for themselves. Those who believe in Jesus Christ will in every way possible honor God by living a righteous life and promote His kingdom here on earth. There is no greater joy in life than to know that one has been called by God to be as a "Light" set upon a hill and bring encouragement and the word of God to his or her fellowman.

All are sinners saved by the grace of God. Through the death, burial, and resurrection of Jesus Christ we have been freed from the bondage of sin and given the opportunity to achieve eternal life through Jesus' sacrifices on the cross of Calvary.

God has given everyone a special gift, which if used properly can help promote His kingdom here on earth. These offerings are intended for that purpose. I encourage the reader to study the word of God as found in the Bible for one year with an open mind and open heart and see the difference it can make in their life.

All Bible references are from the NKJV

Merrill Phillips

THE GLORY OF GOD

Luke 2:14

Glory to God in the highest, and on earth peace, goodwill towards men!

The glory of God surrounds us; we can see His glory everywhere we turn. From the seas to the mountains, His glory is always before us. The heavenly bodies, the seas, the winds, and sky tremble before Him and obey His every command.

Great is the glory of God, both here and in the heavens above, there are none who can compare, there are none who can hide from Him. Those who submit to His will, will enjoy peace here on earth, those who oppose him shall endure his wrath that is to come.

The day will come when Jesus (the Son of God) shall return to earth, all who claim him as King of kings and Lord of lords shall reign with Him forever and ever.

Like his Father, Jesus' glory can be seen from one end of the earth to the other and sin will come to an end, for where His glory prevails sin cannot exist.

All are subject to the power of Jesus, one day even Satan shall acknowledge that Jesus is the Son of God and will stand helpless before Him.

The glory of God lights the way of the righteous and guides them as they walk their road of life.

God will never abandon those who love Him, for that matter He will not abandon those who reject Him, it will be they who abandon Him. God and his glory changes not, man changes with the wind and knoweth not which way to go, he wanders hither and yon, seeking he knoweth not what.

The glory of God will shine round about them and offer peace to all who come to Him and seek His face. God's glory is forever, it never changes.

STRIVING FOR FREEDOM

Galatians 5:1

$\mathcal{S}$tand fast therefore in the liberty by which Jesus has made us free, and do not entangle again with a yoke of bondage.

With the Bible in one hand and the desire to be free in the other nothing can keep us from obtaining freedom.

Freedom from the sins of the world is the desire of all who strive to live a life pleasing to God. It is God who sets the guidelines that must be followed to experience true freedom.

We may live in a free society, free to live as we please, but unless we put God first in our lives we will never know freedom as God intended it to be, mainly free from the sins that pervade this world.

Even freedom does not exempt us from the temptations of sin, but through Jesus Christ, we can avoid the penalty of sin, eternal death.

Through the shedding of Jesus' blood on the cross at Calvary, we were set free to live a life that exemplifies the word of God.

True freedom came from Jesus' sacrificial death, with the wave of His hand, He could have avoided the cross, but His love for you and me was so strong that He allowed His adversaries to put Him to death on a Roman cross.

Three days after his crucifixion Jesus proved the world wrong, death was only the means by which Jesus proved that true freedom lies beyond the grave.

As free as we may live in this life it cannot compare to the freedom that we will experience when we close our eyes in death and awaken to a new life beyond this materialistic life.

While on the cross Jesus opened the door to heaven and has promised all who come to Him will be welcomed in heaven when this life they leave.

Yes, Jesus freed us from the bondage of sin, yes; Jesus set the example for us to follow to obtain true freedom. Yes, Jesus will help us walk the road of life that leads to eternal life and true freedom.

It is true that freedom is not free; it requires us to step out of our boat of comfort and follow the one who can truly set us free, Jesus Christ.

WAITING

1 Corinthians 16:13

*W*atch, stand fast in the faith, be brave, be strong.

Heavenly Father, I pray for the strength and endurance to stand fast in the presence of mine enemies.

Grant unto me the grace to embrace this life without fear of being overcome by the temptations of sin that surround me.

May my days be prosperous, may I comfort those who walk beside me and help them overcome through Your comforting words. May all I do bring glory to Thy name.

As the sun warms the earth and brings forth its fruit, may Your teachings sink deep within me and produce fruit fit for Thy table. May the seeds of this fruit I sow grow and bring comfort to those who struggle with the challenges of this life.

Through Your love O Lord, I will overcome the temptations of this life, temptations that could lead me astray and deliver me into the hands of the great deceiver and be banished from Your sight forever.

Till that day and time I surrender to Thy will. Through surrender I will find solace in Thy word, this will allow me to withstand the onslaught of the great deceiver.

Deep within I can feel the warmth and comfort of Your everlasting love, it quiets my fears and I know that one day I will dwell in Thy presence forever and ever.

I will sing praises unto You, Holy Father; I will seek Thy face throughout the remainder of my life and pray that one day I will rest in Your presence, free from the adversities that now I have to face.

We, Your children anxiously await the return of Your Son, Jesus Christ, as foretold in the scriptures, we will stand fast in Your word and sing praises unto You day and night. Come Lord Jesus, we await Your triumphal return.

JESUS PAID THE PRICE

Hebrews 12:2

ooking unto Jesus, the author and finisher of our faith, who for the joy that was set before Him endured the cross, despising the shame, and has set down at the right hand of the throne of God.

Jesus took our sins upon Himself and paid the price for your sins and mine while nailed to the cross of Calvary. Jesus could have avoided the cross by denying our sins and allowing us to pay the price of sin. However, Jesus' love for you and me was so great that He wants us to spend eternity with Him and He was willing to pay the price of sin for us so that we could avoid being separated from God for eternity.

Jesus opened the door to eternal life and it is up to each one to walk through that door by willingly submitting to the will of God. To submit grudgingly is not acceptable; submission has to be an act we do out of love for our Lord and Savior, Jesus Christ. Jesus is wooing us; it is up to us to respond to His overtures.

The remission of sin requires a sacrifice. Jesus' love for you and me was so great that He stepped forward and allowed Himself to be a sacrifice for the sins of the whole world. In this light, you and I do not have any excuse for not excepting Jesus' sacrifice for ourselves.

It can be argued that there are only a few who accept Jesus' sacrifice for themselves and claim Him as their Savior. The majority may claim to be followers of Jesus but their lives do not reflect that opinion, their deeds give them away.

All are unworthy of the love of God, but through repentance of sin and the desire to follow Jesus we can put into practice qualities that show our desire to become more like Jesus.

No one is or ever will be perfect while living in this sin-filled world. Perfection will come when we enter into our new life beyond the grave and then only those who accepted Jesus Christ as their Lord and Savior will receive that perfection. All others will be cast from God's sight into the lake of fire prepared for Satan and those who reject Jesus Christ as the son of God.

Now is the time to change our ways and turn to the one who can save our soul from the fires of hell (Jesus Christ) and allow Him to be our Lord and Master. He has opened the door to eternal life, it is for us to accept that fact and lovingly submit to His will.

SPRINGTIME, TIME OF RENEWAL

2 Corinthians 4:16

Therefore, we do not lose heart. Even though our outward man is perishing, yet the inward man is being renewed day by day.

Thank you Lord God for this time of year, the cold of winter giving way to the warmth of spring. A sign of God's love towards all of mankind.

Gray and dreary skies give way to cotton-puffy clouds scudding across an azure sky, bringing to mind the beauty of the spring to come.

The ground warmed by the rays of the sun, bringing to life the daffodils and flowering shrubs.

Stirred by the warmth of the early morning sun, lilies sprout and poke their heads above the ground, to display their smiling faces for all to enjoy as lovers stroll down country lanes.

Flowers of spring blooming after a long winter's rest, faces of many different shapes and colors swaying in the gentle breezes of spring.

Wisteria vines display their beauty as their grape cluster like blooms entice one to take time from their busy day and drink in the beauty of spring.

Warm spring rains bring to life the trees of the forest as they dawn their new coats of green.

Birds feather their nests in anticipation of raising their young, nourishing them until they fledge.

The mocking bird practices its repertoire just before the sun drives the night away, adding new and different tunes each day.

Night creatures come to life after the setting of the sun, all stirred to life by the coming of spring, each singing its song of love in hopes of attracting a mate.

Young lovers stroll down lover's lane hand in hand by the light of a full moon, dreaming of a wedding in June.

Springtime, a time of renewal, a time to remember the past and a time to plan for the future, a time to bow before the throne of God and thank Him for another spring.

How It Ought To Be

James 1:5

If any of you lacks wisdom, let him ask of God, who gives to all liberally and without reproach, and it will be given to him.

Come, let us break bread together, let us pray together before we talk and ask God to guide us as we endeavor to settle our differences.

Let us put aside our personal feelings and do the will of God. Let the needs of the people prevail, not what a few want to force down the throat of the public.

There is a middle ground where all parties can agree, seek that rather than self will. Take a lesson from the pages of scripture, lest we divide the people into those who have and those who have not.

It is more important to preserve the union than it is to split this nation into fighting factions where no one wins.

The dissention between those in power and who are not will serve to divide this nation to the point where other nations will look at our behavior and declare, "We do not want to be as they."

We may be the most powerful nation in the world but we are far from being unified. We are more like spoiled children throwing tantrums because we cannot have our own way.

The Bible has the answers to all of our problems but when we turn from the scriptures God will allow us to wallow in our own mud and mire and even allow this nation to become a third world nation.

Today we have contempt for one another where once we had compassion for our fellow Americans.

This is not our world it belongs to God. We are just sojourners here for just a few short years and then we die and we leave hope for a brighter tomorrow or we leave a nation divided.

It is the choice of all Americans as to how we want to live and what kind of government we want to govern us.

If we are wise we will choose the ways of God and live in peace and harmony, be divisive and our days will be full of woe.

Lord Almighty

Ephesians 6:14

Stand therefore, having girded your waist with truth, having put on the breastplate of righteousness.

Oh, how great thou art O Lord, how great thou art.

We are as lost sheep wandering in the darkness of this world, bombarded on all sides by the sin that prevails in this world.

You are our great redeemer Lord Jesus, the protector of our soul; only through You can we prevail against the temptations of Satan.

Though Satan cannot force us to follow him he never gives up trying, You Lord Jesus are our shield against the evil forces of this world.

Without Your truths as our shield surly we would be lost forever without any hope of salvation, but with and through Your word O Lord we can accomplish all things.

Be with us Lord Jesus as we walk our road of life, when dark clouds of sin gather may Your "Light" shine and dispel the sin that hides therein.

Touch our hearts O Lord, that we may come to know You on a personal basis and accept Your word as being the truth that can set us free.

Help us to keep our eye on the day when the clouds of heaven will gather in the east and the trumpets of heaven resound, proclaiming Your return.

Then all wars will cease and Your peace shall prevail, bringing all together with one accord, with one purpose in life, to serve You Lord Jesus.

May all come before your throne and surrender to Your will and live by Your word forevermore, rejoicing that never again will we have to live in fear of losing our struggle against evil.

Only in You and through You Lord Jesus can we live a righteous life, this we acknowledge and strive towards the day that we can proclaim, "I belong to you Lord Jesus, use me for the advancement of Your kingdom here on earth."

THE GREAT I AM

Exodus 3:14

*A*nd God said to Moses, "I AM WHO I AM." And he said, "Thus you shall say to the children of Israel, "I AM has sent me to you."

I AM is his name. He is the one who scattered the stars in the heaven, each and everyone in its proper place. He made the sun to rule by day and the moon by night, mighty is He.

Mighty is He who put the planets in place and put within man the desire to explore the heavens in search of the great I AM.

The shrubs and trees came forth by His word, scattered He the flowers by the roadside and across the land for the enjoyment of man.

The fowl of the air soar on currents of air created by the breath of the great I AM. They soar high above the vastness of the land in search of food to feed their young.

Fish and creatures of the sea swim free in the limitless seas, placed each one He in their proper place, all to be subservient to man.

The beasts of the forest roam free, far and wide roam they in search of their prey. The day will come when the lion will lie down with the lamb and at peace will be they.

Majestic snow capped mountains rise high above the fruited plains, rivers flow across the land and make their way to the sea. On their way, they water the land and bring forth a harvest to quench the appetite of man.

The tides of the world ebb and flow, twice a day they rise and fall to the pleasure of the one who put them in motion, the great I AM.

Man was the special creation of the great I AM, created He them to spend their days in worship of the great I AM.

The great I AM put man in charge of His creation, to till the soil and reap the harvest of the seas. What a gracious God is He.

The great I AM was before the beginning of time, Great is He who sent His only Son, Jesus Christ, to set man free from the sins that keep him from inheriting eternal life offered by the great I AM.

The great I AM was and shall be from the beginning of time and throughout eternity supreme. All who reject Him shall be cast from His sight. All who come to know Him will forsake their evil ways, bow their head and bend their knees before the throne of the great I AM.

ASTER

Matthew 28:6-7

"He is not here; for He has risen as He said. Come; see the place where the Lord lay. "And go quickly and tell His disciples that He is risen from the dead, and indeed He is going before you into Galilee; there you will see Him. Behold I have told you."

As we walk this road of life, we sometimes fall into deep despair. When this happens, remember the cross, the cross where our Lord and Savior, Jesus Christ, died.

Wracked with pain, suffering beyond imagination, Jesus took upon Himself your sins and mine. He paid the price of our disobedience and suffered your pain and mine. Never asking, always giving so that you and I one day can live beyond our earthly ties.

Yes, Jesus made all of this possible by giving His life on the cross at Calvary, by being obedient to His calling, and fulfilling His purpose of coming to earth, being an acceptable sacrifice for the sins of the whole world.

Accept these facts for yourself, take them into your heart, cherish them, live your life accordingly and you too will triumph over the grave. Ignore or disbelieve the Easter story and we will be putting ourselves in danger of being cast into the lake of fire along with Satan and his fallen angels, separated from God for eternity. Come to the cross before death knocks on your door, it is later than you think.

Life here on earth is our opportunity to prepare ourselves for life beyond the grave, Jesus opened the door to heaven to all who will forsake their evil ways and turn their lives over to him. Jesus is our Savior and He gave His life for the sheep of His pasture.

As Easter approaches renew your vow to life a more Christ-like life, one acceptable to God. Only you can prepare yourself for life after death, Jesus set the example, it is our duty to follow in His footsteps and be obedient to His calling.

During the Easter season, we celebrate the death, burial, resurrection and ascension of our Lord and Savior, Jesus Christ. With joy in our hearts for what Jesus did for us on the cross of Calvary we too can join Him in heaven when we close our eyes in death.

PEACE

John 16:33

"These things I have spoken to you, that in Me you may have peace. In the world you will have tribulation, but be of good cheer, I have overcome the world."

Peace comes through Jesus Christ. He came to set us free from the bondage of sin, free to worship God, free to live as pleases Him. Those who choose to follow Jesus Christ are free indeed. Self-indulgence leads to putting self and self-interest before Jesus Christ, thereby negating the love of Jesus that can set us free and change our lives.

Neither God nor Jesus or the Holy Spirit, (being one, the trinity) will never force themselves upon anyone, it is we who have to go before God and ask Him to come into our lives. Then God (the trinity) will respond in a positive way.

There is no greater feeling than to have the Trinity (God the Father, God the Son, and God the Holy Spirit) to enter into one's life and guide one in the way that they should go.

It may not be easy to set one's life long dreams aside and follow someone whom they can neither see nor touch, but to be a true follower of God, that is just what we are asked to do. Through faith in a higher power (God), it can be achieved. The more we trust God the easier it becomes to fulfill His will in our lives. Through submission to the will of God the day will come when it will become second nature to follow God's direction without question.

Then we are free indeed, though bound by the word of God we are freer than we have ever been and we hesitate not to do His bidding. God frees us to bring His word to the lost of this world and bid them to follow the Scriptures and find peace that comes from knowing Jesus Christ as their Lord and Savior.

It can be a formable task and hold many hardships, but when one is working for the Master of the universe they will follow their calling, sometimes even unto death. To lose one's life in service to God is gain.

As we read in the book of John, "Peace I leave with you, My peace I give unto you: not as the world giveth, give I unto you. Let not your heart be troubled, neither let it be afraid."

What more could one ask than to have the assurance of peace as offered by Jesus. He assures us that if we follow Him we will find that peace that we are so desperately looking for.

The Word Of God

Psalm 119:105

*Y*our word is a lamp unto my feet and a light to my path.

Our souls thirsteth for the word of God, the word that can bring us peace, comfort and love as we walk this road of life.

The days may be long, the nights may be short, but the word of God endureth forever, never changing, the same yesterday, today, tomorrow and forevermore.

His word can cleanse the soul of all sin, it can change a disaster into triumph, it never changes as man's word changes, and it is as a healing balm when applied to the trials of life.

God's word comforts the soul as we face the end of this life, it assures us that there is life beyond death, a life free from the sins that now bind us and keeps us from applying the word of God to our lives.

His word can calm an angry sea, silence the raging storm and causes the winds to cease blowing, nature is subject to His command and so is man.

We may be in control of our destiny and live life our way, but when we accept God's word it can change us from a sinner into a saint and assure us that by following His teachings we can spend eternity in His presence.

Though we may be saved by the grace of God we are subject to the consequences of our unrepentant sins, this is the word of God. Like a child seeking the forgiveness and love of its father, so should we seek the love and forgiveness of the most high God.

Some try to change the meaning of God's word and influence others to follow them, but the word of God never changes and will bring wrath upon those who choose to live life their way without regard for the Holy Scriptures.

It is you; it is me who has to transform our lives to conform to the word of God. God's ways and word never changes, man's word and ways change with the wind, and thus he lives an unstable life. Only those who have the word of God in their heart shall endure.

Decision time is now, accept God's word as a guide in thy life and avoid being tormented in the fires of hell for eternity. This life is where we make that decision.

HELP US HOLY FATHER

Psalm 46:1

God is our refuge and strength, a very presence help in trouble.

Comfort us O Lord, Lord of the universe; comfort the sick as they struggle with their afflictions.

Reassure them that You love them and that You really do care, even though the circumstances may say otherwise.

We pray that they will turn to You and seek Your healing touch, bless them almighty God, bless them as only You can.

Touch the heart of those who allow hate to prevail in their lives, Turn their bitterness into songs of praise. That they might see Your "Light" in their darkest hour and kneel before Thy throne in an act of submission.

Blessed be thou O Lord, Lord of the universe and all things therein. We give thanks for the gift of your Son, Jesus Christ, and what He did on our behalf on the cross of Calvary.

We praise Thee O Lord for Your never-ending love and forgiveness. Without it surly we would be cast from Your sight when this world we leave.

We await the return of Your Son Jesus Christ, that we might be worthy to spend eternity with Him. We humble ourselves before Thy throne and will be obedient to Thy word.

Grant us Thy peace and understanding as we struggle with the trials and tribulations we encounter on our road of life.

Help us to remember that You are the reason that we are here and that we owe You our love and devotion and by giving up self we might live a life more pleasing to You.

Through the grace of Your Son, Jesus Christ, we offer our lives to Your service and through His holy name we offer this prayer.

OTHER

Genesis 3:20

*A*nd Adam called his wife's name Eve, because she was the mother of all living.

Mother—The one who gave birth and nursed me when I was born.

Mother—The one I ran to and cuddled in her arms when at night I awoke from a bad dream. She assured me that I would come to no harm.

Mother—The one who nursed me through my childhood diseases, the one who never let me down when I went through the trials of youth.

Mother—The one I ran to when I became frightened, the one who held me tight, kissed me on the forehead and told me everything would be all right.

Mother—The one who carried me to Sunday school and encouraged me to follow the ways of the Lord and taught me to pray every night before I closed my eyes in sleep.

Mother—The one who shed many tears when off to war I went, and cried again the day I came home to stay.

Mother—The one who stood by me when the world thought me wrong, an encouraged me when all others turned their head and said that it could not be done.

Mother—The one who stood tall and proud the day I wed and welcomed my bride as if she was one of her own.

Mother—The one who held her grandson the day that he was born and told the whole world how proud she was to have the family name carried on.

Mother—The one who never complained when sickness overtook her and her life began to fade away.

Mother—The one who told me that she loved me with her last breath just before she went to be with the Lord, on her tombstone I had inscribed, "The Greatest Mother Of All."

Wait Upon The Lord

Psalm 27:14

Wait on the Lord; be of good courage, and he shall strengthen your heart; wait I say, on the Lord.

Heavenly Father, I pray for the strength and endurance to stand fast in the presence of mine enemies.

Grant me the grace to embrace this life without fear of being overcome by the temptations of sin that surround me.

May my days be prosperous, may I comfort those who walk beside me and help them overcome through Your comforting word, may all I do bring glory to Thy name.

As the sun warms the earth and brings forth its fruit, may Your teachings sink deep within me and produce fruit fit for Thy table, may the seed of this fruit grow and bring comfort to those who struggle with the challenges of life.

Through Your love O Lord, I will be able to overcome the temptations of life, temptations that could lead me astray and deliver me into the hands of the great deceiver and be banished from Your sight forever.

Till that day and time I surrender to Thy will, through surrender I will find solace in Thy word. This will enable me to withstand the onslaught of the great deceiver.

Deep within me, I feel the warmth and comfort of Your everlasting love, it quiets my fears and I know that one day I will dwell in Thy presence forever.

I will sing praises unto You, Holy Father; I will seek Thy face throughout the remainder of my life and pray that one day I will rest in Thy presence, free from the adversities that I now face.

We, Your children anxiously await the return of Your Son, Jesus Christ, as foretold in the scriptures. We will stand fast in Your word and sing praises unto You day and night. Come Lord Jesus, we await Your triumphal return.

o To God In Prayer

Philippians 4:6

e anxious for nothing, but in everything in prayer and supplication, with thanksgiving, let your request be made known to God.

As the days and weeks go by the closer to God, we become if we strive to put Him first in our lives.

The art of putting self aside and reaching out for ways to serve others brings us in line with the great commission.

Serving others takes our mind off ourselves, which leaves us free to pray more effectively for those who are in need.

God's love gives us peace in times of trials and tribulation. His love takes the sting out of the disasters of life and leads us closer to Him.

Praying prepares us to accept the will of God in our lives as well as easing the tensions that can manifest themselves in negative ways.

Invested time in prayer is never wasted, it is a way of seeking God's input in our lives and makes us feel better about ourselves.

God is big enough to handle whatever problems we might be facing. He has the answers that we need to straighten out our lives.

Prayer is a way for us to communicate with God, by doing so we become more dependent upon him for our daily needs.

God wants us to come to Him any time of day or night, under all conditions and circumstances. He welcomes the chance to communicate with us while we are on our knees.

God puts no bounds upon what we pray about, all subjects, no matter how big or small we think they might be. He wants us to give them to Him through prayer and relieve ourselves of the burden that they might bring.

Jesus gave us the model prayer that can be found in the book of Matthew 6:9-13, which reads as follows in the KJV version of the Bible. After the manner therefore pray ye: Our Father which art in heaven, hallowed be Thy name, Thy kingdom come, Thy will be done, as it is in heaven. Give us this day our daily bread. And forgive us our debts, as we forgive our debtors. And lead us not into temptation, but deliver us from evil: For thine is the kingdom, and the power, and the glory forever. Amen.

Are You One Of Those

2 Peter 2:1

*B*ut there were also false prophets among the people, even as there will be false teaches among you, who will bring in destructive heresies, even denying the Lord who brought them, and bring on themselves swift destruction.

Be not one of those who say, "I will wait until tomorrow before I pray. I do not have time today."

Be not one of those who say, "I will wait until tomorrow before I seek His will. I do not have time today."

Be not one of those who say, "I will wait until tomorrow before I give myself to the Lord, I am too busy today."

Be not one of those who turn their back on the Lord and promote the will of man. All of those above will one day regret that they turned their back on the Lord above.

Their earthly days may be full of fun with the pleasures of sin, but the day will come when it will all crumble and come caving in.

Then will you hear them cry, "Save me O Lord I pray, save me and I will be yours today."

With a tear in His eye and a frown on His face, the Lord will answer, "Sorry, I called you yesterday and you would not come. You chose sin over Me and now you have to pay."

"Save me O Lord, save me," they will cry. The Lord will reply, "I know thee not, be on thy way."

"Save me O Lord, save me.," they will cry. The Lord will reply, "Where were you when I knocked? I tried, but you were too busy trying to hide."

"Save me." they will cry one last time, and again the Lord will reply, "I know thee not, be on thy way."

As their voices fade away it will be heard, "If only I had it to do over again I would obey and avoid the penalties of my sin. Please Lord let me in."

As they pass from view they will hear, "Sorry, you had a chance, but you refused to change your wicked ways. It was your choice to remain in sin." There will wailing and gnashing of teeth as they face eternity in the fires of hell.

CHRISTIAN FOLLOW ME

Matthew 4:10

Then Jesus said to him, "Away with you, Satan! For it is written, you shall worship the Lord your God, and Him only you shall serve."

Jesus calls across the centuries, "Christians, forsake your wicked ways and follow Me."

When Satan tempts you to stray, tell him, "I haven't time to listen to you; all I have time for is to pray."

Jesus tells us if Satan persists that, we have His permission to use his name against him. If we listen to Satan, he will lead us astray and when he is done with us, he will abandon us and leave us to die in our sins.

Satan is sadistic, selfish and full of greed, clever is he when it comes to deceiving those who live as they please.

Pleasures of the flesh are but for a moment, when it is through it leaves you empty inside. Fulfilling the desires of the flesh leads to nothing but heartache and pain.

Sugar coated temptations may be sweet in the mouth, but when reality sets in they turn bitter in your belly leaving you empty inside with no place to go except to hell and Satan will laugh at you all of the way.

Satan may be the Prince of this world along with those angels who chose to follow him, but the day is coming when they will be bound by the truths of God and thrown into the bottomless pit. There they will remain for a thousand years.

During this time, Jesus will restore peace and harmony throughout the world. Peace and harmony that heretofore we have only dreamed of will become a reality, a prelude of what is to come.

One last time Satan and his angels will be released from the bottomless pit just before they are thrown into the lake of fire where the worm never dies. There, he and all who have followed him will be tormented forever and ever. Never again, to interfere in the lives of those who choose to follow Jesus Christ.

Now you know the rest of the story. A sad story indeed, but one that will come true for all who point their finger at God and say, "I do not need You or Your Son, Jesus Christ, or the Holy Spirit in my life. Go away and leave me alone."

$\mathcal{A}$ Cross On A Far Away Hill

Hebrews 12:2

$\mathcal{L}$ooking unto Jesus, the author and finisher of our faith, who for the joy that was set before Him endured the cross, despising the shame, and has set down at the right hand of the throne of God.

With light from above, I go there every night in hopes of seeing my Lord on high.

To receive from Him the blessings that will carry me through the hard days that lie ahead.

His blessings give me the assurance that I am not alone in a world that tries to hold me at bay.

When I see that cross, I know that He loves me and I need not worry what this world can do to me.

If I keep my eyes on the cross, one day I will be able to enjoy the freedom that it represents for those who follow Jesus.

A greater joy no one can have than the sight of that cross on that far away hill.

It gives me hope when all hope is gone of surviving the ills of this world.

The "Light" from that cross burns deep within my soul and I can feel its love and warmth on days when things go wrong.

A greater sight my eyes will never behold than the cross on that hill far away.

AMONG THE FLOWERS

Isaiah 40:8

*T*he grass withers, the flower fades, but word of our God stands forever.

Walking in the garden among the flowers, I find peace and tranquility.

In the garden of Gethsemane, I find the love that Jesus Christ left there for me.

At night when I bend my knees and pray I find security in the knowledge that God is listening to me.

At dawn when I awake, I search the eastern sky for clouds that will announce the coming of our Lord and Savior, Jesus Christ. They will remind me that one day Jesus will return and release me from the trappings that now bind me.

During the heat of the day, I recall the Exodus and the hardships that Moses and his people had to face.

For forty years, they wandered from place to place before they crossed over Jordon and entered into the land of milk and honey.

In the cool of the evening I talk with God and confess my daily sins, I repent and prepare for the coming of a new day.

What I enjoy the most is the time spent among the flowers, communing with God and seeking His grace.

We, like the flowers, have our day in the sun. A time to leave our mother's womb, a time to live and seek the grace of God. A time to die and return to God so that our children can have their time and place in God's creation.

E Lives

Job 19:25

*F*or I know that my redeemer lives, and He shall stand at last on the earth.

They drove three old rusty nails through my Lord and into the cross at Calvary. One through each hand, one through His feet, these three old rusty nails represents your sins and mine.

Our Lord Jesus took your sins and mine upon Himself and paid the penalty that belonged to you and me.

His love for us was strong enough to sustain Him in His hour of need, never again will we have to hang our head in shame and hide in our place of secret.

From that time till this Jesus has invited all to come before His throne where we can receive forgiveness of our sins and warm our souls in the warmth of his love.

Our Lord and Savior may have died on the cross of Calvary, but on the third day, He arose from the grave and settled for all time that sin and death has no power over a righteous man.

When Satan's temptations come tell him that you have given your life to Jesus Christ and are no longer under his control.

Invite Satan to join you before the throne of Jesus Christ and I assure you that he will flee from you and seek another who has yet to turn to Jesus.

Great will be the day when Jesus returns to this sin-filled world and establish His kingdom here on earth.

Graves will open and Saints shall rise triumphal over death and join in signing praises unto His holy name.

With His pierced hands and feet, He will shower His love upon all who kneel before Him and surrender their lives to His service.

Death, sin, sickness, disease and Satan will surrender to the power of the one who created everything, Jesus Christ, and everything will become new.

Jesus lives, His redemptive work on the cross has saved us from the fires of hell. Go before His throne and devote the rest of your live to Him.

ETERNAL LIFE

1 Timothy 6:12

*F*ight the good fight of faith, lay hold on eternal life, to which you were also called and have confessed the good confession in the presence of many witnesses.

Out of the hand of Satan comes the trials of life, trials that Satan hopes will distract us from following the path that leads to eternal life, such as earthly wealth as the main goal in our life or the fulfillment of self-desires over spiritual achievements.

Curse not God for the trials of life, but rather praise Him for sending his Son, Jesus Christ, to be a sacrifice for our sins. God will provide the necessary strength and knowledge to overcome any and all temptations that Satan puts in our way.

God knows our limits and will intervene on our behalf when we turn to Him and submit ourselves to His will rather than our own. Our way can lead to the gates of hell while God's way leads to peace and harmony.

Peace is the product of submitting ourselves to the will of God and putting Him first in our lives. With peace comes contentment and with contentment comes the desire to serve our living Lord and Savior, Jesus Christ, with accepting Jesus Christ comes eternal life.

Eternal life is the greatest reward that can be bestowed upon anyone. It is bestowed upon those who forsake the ways of the flesh and strive to live a more Christ-like life, a life reflecting the attributes of God.

To strive to live a more Christ-like life is a noble cause indeed, one worthy of whatever sacrifice one has to make to achieve that end. Many try but only a few shall achieve.

Without Jesus Christ in our lives, this life has little to offer but heartache and pain. Though we may achieve much wealth and power in the end they are but hollow victories, victories that vanish when we pass from this life. All of the wealth and power in this world cannot buy eternal life, it is a gift from God to those who choose to follow Him.

Satan clouds the mind of man and will do all that he can to keep us from accepting Jesus Christ as our Lord and Savior, his ways are subtle and destructive. Satan's agenda is to keep as many of God's created beings (you and me) from accepting Jesus Christ as their Lord and Savior as possible, thus keeping them from inheriting eternal life.

Each person has to make the decision to follow Jesus Christ or Satan. To live for Christ may require one to live a life of poverty and self-sacrifice, but in the end, that one will receive eternal life. Those who choose to live a self-fulfilled life without Jesus as their Lord and Savior shall reap the rewards of the wicked, eternity in hell.

Eternal life is sought by many, but only a few shall achieve it, eternal life requires the acceptance of Jesus Christ as God's one and only Son, our Lord and Savior. No other way is possible.

WORKING FOR GOD

Matthew 26:41

"Watch and pray, lest you enter into temptation. The spirit indeed is willing, but the flesh is weak."

Man's work for God, no matter how well intentioned cannot have any corrupt stones in its foundation. Just one greedy person in the chain of command can derail all of the good intentions of the rest.

God represents perfection, therefore all involved in a just and righteous endeavor must comply to a higher standard.

Without such compliance the noblest intentions will fail, all evil must be removed before God will allow great things to happen in His name where man is involved.

An organization based on a crumbing foundation will never stand and when it falls, it will destroy the most ardent of souls.

It is better not to start a noble project than to have it fail and have the failure blamed on innocent people who have a righteous heart.

Evil is rampant in this world and temptations great, especially when it comes to money and power.

It is better to die a pauper in the eyes of the world and have a heart tempered by the love of God, than to die the richest and most powerful person in the world under the sadistic control of Satan. Neither wealth nor power can buy one moment of peace or one iota of God's love.

Be at peace with what you have and kneel before the throne of God in submission to His will and He will bless you and supply you with your every need.

Wealth and power is not the answer to our earthly problems, God is the answer to the conflicts of the mind and soul.

With God and His will fulfilled in our lives we can accomplish anything that is noble and to the benefit of our fellowman.

Become as servants willing to give your lives to the cause that God has called you to fulfill and success will follow. Rely on self and worldly power and failure is assured. Many there are who fall to the temptations of the world and lose their rightful place in God's kingdom.

THANKSGIVING

Psalm 100:4

Enter into His gates with thanksgiving, and into His courts with praise. Be thankful to Him, and bless His name.

T— Take time every day to thank God for all of the blessings that He bestows upon you daily.

H— How is your relationship with Jesus Christ? He gave His life for you, now give your life to His service.

A— Always, but always confer with Jesus Christ before you make any final decisions concerning the matters of life.

N— Never let a day go by without acknowledging that Jesus Christ is your Lord and Savior.

K— Knowing that you know that you will spend eternity with Jesus Christ is a worthy goal in life.

S— Saying thanks for all of your blessings is not enough, allow Jesus to become your personal guide as you walk through this life.

G— Giving of yourself to the work of the kingdom of God is more noble than gaining all the wealth in the world.

I— In as much as we are children of God, it is our duty to become more like Him in all we say and do.

V— Very few who claim to be Christians live a life that exemplifies the virtues of Jesus Christ.

I— Identify yourself with a God fearing church and reach out to those who are in need and make a difference in their lives.

N— Now is the time to accept Jesus Christ into your life and turn from your sinful ways.

G— Going in the wrong direction? Stop, turn around and walk with a humble heart to the foot of the cross and give your life to the one gave you life, Jesus Christ.

TRUST

Proverbs 3:5

$\mathcal{T}$rust in the Lord with all your heart, and lean not on your own understanding.

Trust in God, turn your life over to Him, let Him know what is bothering you and He will provide answers to your problems.

It may not seem natural to put your trust in someone you can neither see nor touch, for God is spirit, although He is seen in and through His only Son, Jesus Christ.

Jesus said, "I am the way, the truth, and the life. No one comes to the Father except through Me." Jesus wants us to trust Him in all circumstances. Jesus wants us to come to Him in good times as well as bad.

When things in your life go wrong put your trust in Jesus Christ and He will take the fear out of what is confronting you. He will guide you as you go through the trials that you face on a daily basis.

The "Light" of Jesus Christ shines on our pathway of life; it lights our way and makes it easier to walk the pathway that lies before us.

Being with Jesus is our ultimate goal, adhering to His word makes the journey of life that much easier. With the fear of failure gone we can walk towards our final goal without the fear of failure.

Jesus wants all to come to Him and to depend upon Him while walking their journey of life.

Turn to Jesus while it is still day, for the hour approaches when all will face their day of judgment, this will be the day that we will have to account as to how we conducted our lives.

Those who turned to Jesus and trusted Him in all matters of life will have no fear; all others will tremble and quake in their boots as they are denied entrance into the presence of God.

Those who deny Jesus Christ will receive the damnation of hell as their reward for not trusting Jesus and allowing Him to be a part of their lives.

Trust and obey is the logo of all who can see beyond tomorrow and know trusting Jesus in all aspects of life they will be spared the torture of eternal denial.

Healing Balm

Matthew 24:13

*B*ut he who endures to the end shall be saved.

The love of God is as a healing balm for the nations of the world. Though we may still have problems and still submit to sin, they can be overcome through a greater understanding of God's love.

Through the study of and the application of God's love to our lives, we can overcome sin and grow in God's wisdom and grace.

Giving up self-interest for the benefit of our fellowman reflects the attributes of God in our lives. Reaching out in love instead of war, we can bring healing where there was once strife.

Strife brings turmoil; love brings peace, not only peace but also, healing and a better understanding of how God's love works in our lives.

If allowed, God's love can bring peace to nations that have been at odds with their neighbors for generations. God and His love is the answer to problems of generations of the past to generations yet to be born.

God's Son, Jesus Christ, proved His love towards His creation by giving Himself as a sacrifice for the sins of the whole world.

We need not fear of what is to come if we accept God's love for ourselves and live a life according to God's will, mainly by putting Him first in our lives.

When the love of God is expressed through our behavior sin cannot prevail in our lives, but where the lack of God's love is expressed, strife shall follow.

God promised that all who put Him first in their lives peace shall prevail. When sin raises its ugly head God's love can keep sin from prevailing in our lives.

Through searching the scriptures, one can glean the truths that can encourage one to submit to the will of God, thus allowing the healing balm of God to restore peace and harmony in our lives.

To he who endures to the end shall reap great rewards in heaven when they leave this life behind and enter into the kingdom of God.

TIME

Ecclesiastes 3:2

time to be born, and a time to die; a time to plant, and a time to pluck what is planted.

God has allotted us just so much time to live on earth, time enough to come to know Him and believe in His Son, Jesus Christ and spread the good news.

Many there are who waste their time chasing the things that are pleasing to the flesh and ignoring the one who created them, God, through His Son, Jesus Christ.

Much to their dismay, they will not be allowed to enter heaven on their own or their earthly deeds, no matter how great they may be.

Only through Jesus Christ (God's Son), can anyone come to God and spend eternity with Him.

T— Time on earth is limited, use it wisely, include, loving your neighbor as yourself.

I— Interaction within the family of God expresses love one for the other.

M— Me and self is insignificant compared to giving of our time in service to God and others.

E— Eternity awaits all of us, some to eternal life, some to eternal damnation.

A Love Story

Deuteronomy 6:5

You shall love the Lord your God with all of your heart, with all of your soul, and with all of your strength.

There is a place in my heart that can only be filled by You, O Lord. Whether morning, noon, or night You fill my heart with joy, My whole day revolves around You.

When skies are gray and my soul is burdened with cares, I recall our relationship and I am no longer blue.

There are times when I anticipate hearing You call my name while walking a woodland path, taking in the beauty of Your creative hand.

While traveling across moonlit-crusted snow on a cold winter's night, I stay warm just thinking of You.

You are without a doubt the best thing that has ever happened to me, You express Your love and care in so many different ways. You are always near, ready to extend a helping hand, and You supply my every need, great and small.

No one has ever loved me so; You support me in everything I do. You do not always approve everything I do, but You love me anyway and tell me that I belong to you.

When I turn my head and go the other way, You patiently wait until I see the error of my ways and turn again to You.

You know the very depths of my soul and yet You hesitate not to share Your love for me. I will never know how someone as loving as You can put up with someone like me.

Whenever I mention Your name some people shun and turn the other way, saying, "If I were you I wouldn't waste my time." in referring to my relationship with You.

You know what? I wouldn't have it any other way, I love You Jesus and I will do all I can to help reconcile others to You.

Lord Jesus give me the strength and courage and I will spend the rest of my life planting the seeds of love among the wolves, asking nothing for myself, except to serve You.

GENERATION TO GENERATION

Revelation 20:12

*A*nd I saw the dead, small and great, standing before God, and books were opened. And another book was opened, which is the BOOK OF LIFE, and the dead were judged according to their works, by the things which were written in the books.

When this life I leave, Lord Jesus take me by the hand and console me as through the door of death I walk.

That I may stand tall and hold my head high as I listen for my name to be called from the Book of Life.

Blot out my sins and wash me clean in the blood of the Lamb, that my soul might be worthy to spend eternity with Thee.

That I might walk the streets of gold and drink of the water that flows from Thy throne, and eat of the fruit of the Tree of Life.

Grant peace to the generations that are yet to come, guide them as You have guided me. Speak to their hearts as they struggle to do Thy will in their lives.

Open the door so that Thy "Light" may be as a beacon of hope unto their souls and a "Light" unto their path.

As their time comes to leave, their earthly home grant them the privilege of spending eternity with Thee.

Grant O Lord from generation to generation that Thy love might shine through the clouds of sin and be as a lighthouse with its light searching in the darkness of night for all who are lost in the sea of sin.

May Your love, Your peace, Your comfort and forgiveness be to all generations until the return of Your Son, Jesus Christ. These things we ask in His Holy Name, Amen.

REVIVAL

Hebrews 11:6

*B*ut without faith it is impossible to please Him, for he who comes to God must believe that He is, and that He is a rewarder of those who diligently seek him.

R— Real love, compassion, and grace comes from God and will sustain us as we walk the straight and narrow path that leads to eternal life.

E— Every day is one day closer to the day when Jesus Christ will return.

V— Very soon the clouds will gather in the east, when least expected there Jesus will be.

I— In the wink of an eye we will be changed, we will see Jesus as He is and we will be like Him.

V— Victory over sin will be ours when we turn to Jesus and let Him have His way in our lives.

A— All are welcomed in the kingdom of God, for God wants no one left behind.

L— Live and conduct yourselves as if it was your last day before you meet Jesus face to face.

DIVINE PROTECTION

Isaiah 9:2

The people who walk in darkness have seen a great light; those who dwell in the land of the shadow of death, upon them a light has shined.

Lord Jesus that You will keep us safe by night and day. When the sun goes down and we are surrounded by the darkness of night, light up the heavens so that we will not stumble and fall prey to the sins that lurk in the darkness of life.

Awake us at the break of day so that at the rising of the sun we can see the beauty of a newborn day, for each day You paint the eastern sky colors pleasing to the eye of man.

When the storm clouds of life gather and the thunder of sin roars, cover us with Your protective hand and keep us from falling prey to Satan's deceitful ways.

When the day comes when we close our eyes in death O Lord, we pray that we will open them beyond the grave and see all of the worlds that You have made.

Though there will be those who grieve our passing, we will rejoice as we enter into Paradise where You now reign with peace and love.

This wicked world with all its sinful ways we will have left behind to begin life anew under Your divine protection.

O Lord there will never be another You, one who cares and loves us regardless how deep the sin we indulge in.

Only in and through You O Lord can we survive this wicked world and come to say, "Thank You Lord for the divine protection You provided for those who believe."

Until You come again Lord Jesus hold Your protective hand over those who strive to live a life pleasing to You.

We pray for the day that we will be able to shout, "Glory, Alleluia, today is the day that we have been waiting for, the day that You will stand in the clouds for the whole world to see and come to know that You truly are Lord of lords and King of kings."

Seek Ye The Lord

Psalm 63:1

O God, You are my God; early will I seek You; my soul thirsts for you; my flesh longs for You in a dry and thirsty land where there is no water.

God of the universe, Father of us all, creator of all that we observe, grant us peace, wisdom and understanding.

Open the scriptures to us, that we might have a greater understanding of Your ways.

Holy Father, grant unto us courage and strength to go through the fires of life as they burn off the dross that keeps us from Your side.

As we touch, the lives of others give unto us the wisdom and knowledge to influence them in a positive way. May our lifestyle be an incentive for them to want to seek You in their times of need.

Not that we are perfect or anywhere near it, but that we have a personal relationship with You and seek You when we ourselves are confronted with the temptations of Satan.

It is only through Your gift of strength, wisdom and courage that we ourselves are able to overcome the adversities of life.

We thank You O Lord for loving us so much that You sent Your Son, Jesus Christ, to take our place on the cross of Calvary. Jesus was obedient to His calling and hesitated not to give his life as a sacrifice for your sins and mine, in doing so He set us free from the bondage of sin.

Jesus, the one who provided us a way to forgive our enemies and the ability to reach out to all with the holy love that flows from Your throne.

We, Your followers humbly thank You Lord God for sending your Son as a sacrifice for our sins, so that we might spend eternity with You.

We pray in the name of Your Son, Jesus Christ.

$\mathcal{H}$IS HEALING HAND

Isaiah 53:5

$\mathcal{B}$ut He was wounded for our transgressions, He was bruised, for our iniquities; the chastisement for our peace was upon Him, and by His stripes we are healed.

O gracious Lord, Father of us all, may Your love be with us as we go day to day.

Peace of mind is one of Your great gifts, we learn to depend upon you in our times of need. It is only through the sacrifices of your Son, Jesus Christ, that we have any hope of eternal life.

As we patiently await His return, we are preparing ourselves for such an event by searching the scriptures and applying them to our lives. No matter at what stage of spiritual growth we are at, none of it would be possible without Your love and guidance.

It is with thankful hearts and open minds that we seek to fulfill what You have called us to do, through our desire to be more like Jesus we grow closer to You.

At times, we feel alone on our journey through this life, but when we turn to You we become aware that You will be with us all through our journey of life.

After going through the trials and tribulations of life, we can look back and see that we were being refined like silver and gold when it goes through the smelting pot where the dross is burned away and only the pure metal is left.

In this process, we leave our old sinful ways behind and look forward to a life that is more pleasing to You, one that reflects the attributes of Jesus Christ.

At times it is hard to see beyond our sinful ways because they are usually pleasing to the flesh and seemingly harmless, but once pointed out we can see just how cleaver Satan is in his deceitful ways.

We beseech Thee O Lord to heal and comfort the sick and impaired, that they might turn to You and seek your comfort in their times of need.

With grateful hearts, we seek to do Thy will and will praise You always as you touch our lives with Your healing hand. We praise Your Son, Jesus Christ, for His sacrifices on our behalf.

A New Day

Psalm 118:24

*T*his is the day that the Lord has made; we will rejoice and be glad in it.

We will awaken to a new day when this life on earth fades away. When the clouds of death draw near turn to Jesus and with an outstretched hand, He will greet you.

Jesus will welcome us as one by one we leave this life behind and the sun rises on our new life beyond the grave.

Home to stay we will be when through the door of death we precede. The clouds of sin will fade away, sights never before seen will brighten our day.

We will hear the Master's voice and feel the love that He will share with the repentant soul as we enter His sheepfold.

Without fear or trepidation we will walk and talk with our heavenly host, neither shy nor bold we will be as we dwell in His presence forevermore.

Peace will reign and never more will we hang our head in shame the day that we embark on our trip to our heavenly home.

Sorrow not over the death of a loved one, but rather rejoice that they are in the presence of Jesus Christ, never again to live under the influence of sin.

Love and peace awaits us as we awaken to a new day beyond the grave.

 Friend Indeed

Proverbs 18:24

man who has friends must himself be friendly, but there is a friend that sticks closer than a brother.

How could I be so blind that I could not see that all it takes is just one friend to make a difference in my life.

Without that one friend surly, I would not now be free, free to worship the one who changed me from a sinner to a saint in the wink of an eye.

By myself, I could not change my ways, but by meeting, my best friend in the whole world will explain how and why I changed my ways.

Should you be in search of a change, may I introduce you to the one who made a difference in my life.

He came into this world over two thousand years ago through a virgin birth, which was never heard of before or since.

He taught His Father's word and opened the door to heaven and eternity; He opened them to all who come to believe that He is who He claims to be.

Yes, it is Jesus Christ, God's only begotten Son who came to earth to set us free from the influence of Satan and his dastardly deeds.

When He was rejected and nailed to the cross at Calvary, His blood washed us clean of the sins of the world, and then He returned to His Father's side where he now resides.

He not only set us free, He also set things right with God so that when this world we leave we will be able to enter heaven without one plea.

Yes, it was Jesus Christ who changed my life, He can do the same for you, open your heart to him and accept Him as your Lord and Savior and see.

BLOOD OF THE LAMB

Revelation 1:5

And from Jesus Christ, the faithful witness, the first born from the dead, and the ruler over the kings of the earth. To Him who loved us and washed us from our sins in His own blood.

The blood of Jesus Christ still heals today, though He gave His life on that cross many long years ago He still lives in our hearts today.

With every drop of blood that fell while Jesus was on the cross many were blessed, Jesus left a legacy that will never be suppressed.

His shed blood triumphed over sin and set you and me free from the bondage of sin. What a comfort that is to all who believe.

As His blood dripped to the ground it shook the foundation of the world, nothing remained the same. He came meek and mild as a lamb; He restored the faith of man, and set us all free.

Jesus suffered the fate of man, when He left He promised that one day He would return. A faithful few stand guard and wait for the heavens to open and reveal His triumphal return.

All who gather at the foot of the cross will benefit from the shed blood of the Lamb. The shed blood of Jesus transcends the transgressions of man; it purifies the soul and redeems fallen man.

Unless we walk by faith and faith alone we will miss the blessings that Jesus has in store for those who bathe in the blood of the lamb.

It wasn't yesterday, it isn't tomorrow, it is today that we are asked to turn to Jesus and profess Jesus as our Savior and the Son of God throughout the land.

Immerse thyself in the shed blood of the Lamb and become white as snow, glorified, sanctified, and purified. A child of God, awaiting Jesus' return.

Glory to God for allowing Jesus Christ to live among sinful fallen man and for opening the door that leads to the resurrection of man.

The shed blood of the Lamb was for the glorification of man.

LIKE JESUS

Deuteronomy 6:13

"*You* ou shall fear the Lord your God and serve Him, and shall take oaths in His name.

Dear lord Jesus thank you for Your loving care, for Your sacrifice on the cross so that I might be free from the bondage of sin.

I have a great desire to be an extension of Your hand, to be an example to others of Your love.

To do Your will in my life and to be a ray of hope to those whom I encounter day by day.

To minster to my fellow workers in a way that they might have a desire to seek You and live a life more pleasing to You.

Instill in their hearts a desire to turn from temptation and replace it with a desire to walk in Your footsteps.

That most of all I might be as a shinning "Light" in the clouds of darkness and sin, a "Light" that others might follow into the sunshine of Your love.

Use me O Lord in whatever capacity that is pleasing to You, lead me O Lord and I will follow and give to You all of the honor and praise that others might direct towards me.

Loving Jesus, we come before Thy throne and ask that You guide us as we travel the road of life and grant that when this life is over that we might spend eternity in Your presence.

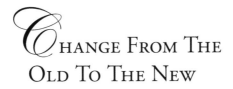

CHANGE FROM THE OLD TO THE NEW

Romans 6:6

Knowing this, that our old man was crucified with Him, that the body of sin might be done away with, that we should no longer be slaves of sin.

Over here Lord, please show me how to change from the old to the new, it seem impossible for me to do. Where do I start, where do I stop?

I cannot see Lord how to change from the old to the new. My eyes are clouded Lord, and my glasses are fogged up too.

The words of scripture are not clear to me Lord; please show me what to do. I try and try again Lord, but still I cannot quite see what to do. Please show me just once more that which I should do.

This time I will wipe away the mist that clouds my vision, but the mist still prevails and yet it is beginning to fade away. At times, it returns and I cannot quite see, that is without Your hand to wipe the mist away.

The darkness that surrounds me O Lord is not where I want to be; in the darkness Lord, I cannot see how to change from the old to the new.

O Lord please send Your Son unto me, for I knows that He will be able to show me how to change from the old to the new. I await Thee Lord to clear the mist that surrounds me, and then I will know what to do.

At last Lord, I am beginning to see; now I can take the first step Lord as Your "Light" begins to shine in my life. The more You wipe my tears away Lord the clearer things become to me.

I know that it will not be long now Lord before I will be able to clearly see how to change from the old to the new.

Your ways are new to me O Lord, yet they are as old as time. "The way that I showed you my child comes from the love that I have for you. Hold it dear my child and pass it on to someone new, so that they too will learn how to change from the old to the new."

Thank You O Lord for Your loving care and for showing us all how to change from the old to the new.

Let It Be Said

1 Peter 5:6

Therefore humble yourselves under the mighty hand of God, that He may exalt you in due time.

I would like it be said of me that God saved him from spending eternity in hell when he turned from his disobedient ways and sought the solace of God. That he was an obedient child of God and that he allowed God to guide him on his of road of life.

That he took up his cross and followed Jesus Christ, that he sought the comfort of God as he went through his trials of life. That he resisted the temptations of Satan by holding fast to the word of God.

Let it be said that he sought the comfort that God offers all as the fires of life burned away the dross that brought him closer to God instead of seeking revenge for the wrongs that were imposed upon him.

That he humbled himself before the throne of God and thought of himself more of a servant of God, rather than one seeking glory for himself, of how honored he felt when God told him, "Take pen and paper and write." and left the rest up to him.

Of how humble he walked before God and gave God all of the credit for his literary accomplishments, for he himself was unschooled in that field and wrote only that which God lead him to put on paper.

That he lived a long fulfilled life, that he reached out to others through his writings and encouraged them to seek the word of God and apply it to their lives, for in the end that is all that really matters in this life.

If you would like these things said about you when you have gone then turn to God now and turn your life over to Him and allow Him to guide you on your road of life. Let God lead you to what He wants you to do rather than what you want. Become a servant of God rather than a servant of self-desire.

It is a matter of what one thinks is more important in life, fulfilling self-desires or preparing oneself for the life that comes after death of the flesh. By following, what God has for you to do it will be said of you that you were a faithful servant of the most high God.

I humbly offer this as a testimony of what God can do in one's life if they are willing to forego some of the pleasures of life and be obedient to God's calling.

PLANTING SEEDS OF LOVE

1 Corinthians 3:6-8

I planted, Apollos watered, but God gave the increase. So then neither he who plants is anything, nor he who waters, but God who gives the increase. Now he who plants and he who waters are one, and each one will receive his own reward according to his own labor.

Plant your seeds of love, water them with wisdom from the scriptures and your garden of life will flourish.

Mind not the weeds of unrighteousness that grow among your flowers of love, in the last days they will be separated from the fruits of your labor and cast from your sight forever.

Be gentle with those who are just beginning their walk with Jesus lest they turn from their spiritual growth and be lost forever.

Encourage others to turn to Jesus in their times of troubles and in their good times, for to turn from Him will only result in falling prey to the evil one, condemned to spend eternity separated from God forever.

Cultivate your garden of love, water it with the waters of holiness and forgiveness and it will bring forth fruit fit for God's table.

All are scarred by their works of sin, turn to Jesus and seek His forgiveness and He will heal you and set you back on the path of righteousness.

Toiling for Jesus may not produce earthly riches, but your soul will grow beyond all expectations and treasures without price will await you in heaven above.

Through all seasons of life, praise the Lord Jesus for what He did while here on earth, especially for paying the price for your sins and mine on the cross of Calvary, setting us free from the bondage of sin.

Jesus plowed the fields of humanity and planted the seeds of righteousness, watered them with heavenly love so that we might reap the benefits of His labor and by so doing spend eternity with Him.

Go before the throne of God and offer yourself to His service and He will supply everything you will need to fulfill what He wants you to do.

There is a time to plant, a time to water, and a time to harvest. Be willing to let God use you in whatever capacity He chooses and your life will have meaning.

DOOR TO ETERNITY

John 10:9-10

I am the door. If anyone enters by Me, he will be saved, and will go in and out and find pasture. The thief does not come except to steal, and to kill, and to destroy, I have come that they might have life, and that they may it more abundantly.

To stay in this sin filled world is pain, to depart and be with Jesus Christ surly will be gain.

We live day by day with heartache and pain, whereas one day Jesus will console our soul as we pass from life to eternal life.

When in Jesus' presence we dwell we will be free to walk the streets of gold and eat of the fruit of the tree of life, never again to witness cruelty of man towards man.

Our soul will be at peace, never wanting to return to this

sin-filled world, there will be life eternal where once there was death and shame.

Life unto life, glory unto glory, Jesus Christ will be in control and sin will be no more.

Satan will have been banned from troubling the heart of man, for in the lake of fire he will stand, tormented by the fires of hell, along with all who accept his will.

Satan could have changed and received forgiveness of his sins against humanity, but stubborn was he; in the lake of fire, he will pay the price.

Follow not Satan to the pits of hell, but rather, change your ways through the blood of the Lamb, Jesus Christ, and you will live in peace and harmony with your fellowman.

Take your place in God's plan of redemption, for those who forsake their sinful ways, peace, harmony, and eternal life will be their reward for accepting Jesus Christ as their door to eternity.

THANK YOU JESUS

Galatians 6:14

But God forbid that I should boast except in the cross of our Lord Jesus Christ, by whom the world has been crucified to me, and I to the world.

My soul will find rest in heaven, for Jesus has told me so, rest that I now do not know.

Jesus is the one that my soul thirsteth for, He is the Lord of my life, and no one else will do.

As Jesus hung on the cross of Calvary He washed me white as snow with his own shed blood.

There is no other place that I had rather be than at the foot of the cross at Calvary.

Thank You Lord Jesus for taking my place on the cross at Calvary so that when I pass from this life I will be able to spend eternity with Thee.

The day that I join Thee Lord Jesus, free from my sins I will be. Jesus, the greatest name I know, I will follow Thee wherever I may go.

Jesus will lead me, this I know because the Bible tells me so. Astray I will never go if I keep my eyes on Jesus and His ways always before me.

I will follow Him all the way to heaven when this earth I leave, there He has prepared a place for me, for the Bible tells me so.

Jesus, Jesus, the sweetest name I know, He will always be my Savior, from His lips I have heard Him say so,

It is not for all to understand, just believe and you too will be free from the sins that now bind you.

Great is the love of Jesus for you and for me, he loves us even though our sins are an affront to Him.

Thank You Jesus for dying for the sins of the world and setting us free, free to join Thee when this world we leave.

FATHER

Genesis 2:24

*T*herefore a man shall leave his father and mother and be joined to his wife, and they shall become one flesh.

F— Is for Forever; Forever he is devoted to his wife and his family, ever faithful and trustworthy.

A— Is for Active; Active, interested, and helpful in his families activities, sets a good example for them to follow.

T— Is for Tireless; Tireless in sharing his time in the upbringing of his children.

H— Is for Handy; Handy around the house to fix household problems without complaining.

E— Is for Encourage; Encourages his wife in her efforts of

rearing their children, sets a good example in the families religious life.

R— Is for Ready; Ready to give a helping hand and to witness to those in need.

DEATH ON THE CROSS

John 11:25-26

*J*esus said to her, "I am the resurrection and the life. He who believes in Me, though he may die, he shall live. And whoever lives and believes in Me shall never die. Do you believe this?"

Many long years ago, they nailed my Savior to a cross at Calvary.

They scourged Him and platted a crown of thorns and put it on His brow.

He was silent as He stood before Pilate, the crowd convicted him and Pilate turned Him over to them to be crucified.

They convicted Him because He claimed to be the Son of God, so Pilate yielded to their demands.

One by one, they drove three rusty nails through His flesh into the cross at Calvary.

As He hung on the cross that day, He cried unto God, "Forgive them Father, for they know not what they do."

The crowd stood all around and laughed at Him as His blood dripped to the ground. They proclaimed, "Others He saved, himself he cannot, come down from that cross and we will believe."

The day that Jesus died on the cross at Calvary He overcame the sins of the world and set us free.

From the top to the bottom, the veil of the temple tore in two, thus allowing us to have a personal relationship with God above.

Then they placed Jesus' body in a grave, but no grave on earth could hold the Son of God. On the third day, He arose from the grave and talked to quite a few.

Before He ascended into heaven He consoled His disciples and proved to Thomas that He was who He claimed to be.

$\mathcal{B}$E READY

Matthew 24:30

$\mathcal{T}$hen the sign of the Son of Man will appear in heaven, and then all of the tribes of the earth will mourn, and they will see the Son of Man coming on the clouds of heaven with power and great glory.

Jesus is not on that cross anymore, He now resides by His Father's side. He paid the price for the sins of mankind before He left this earth behind.

Jesus is preparing a new place for you and me, when He comes again, He will be as the great Shepherd and lead His flock home.

Before He left this world He commanded us to tell all people of this world about His great love for them and how one day He would return and take unto Himself His own.

Whether it be in your hometown or halfway around the world, be bold, tell everyone of the great love that awaits those who believe in God's only Son, Jesus Christ.

When the clouds gather in the east keep a watchful eye on the sky, for one day there He will be; with outstretched arms calling to you and me, "Come, follow Me."

On that glorious day the righteous shall rise and meet Him in the sky, first from the grave and then those who now reside on this cosmic planet He put in place among the stars of the sky.

In His voice will be nothing but love and compassion for all who believe, the rest will run and hide in the cracks and rills of the hills, hoping He will not see the fear in their eyes.

Knowing all things Jesus will give them one more chance to change their minds and stand with Him instead of following Satan to the lake that burns with fire and the worm never dies.

Like the great Shepherd that He is, His sheep will know His voice and obey His every command, praying for their fellowman as they leave this world behind.

Jesus lives in the hearts of all who believe and when He returns He will find them waiting, with a great shout all will say, "All glory and power belongs to Jesus the Christ, the Son of our living God."

God's Light

John 1:5

This is the message which we have heard from Him and declare it to you, that God is light and in Him is no darkness at all.

God's "Light" drives all sin away, in His "Light" sin cannot survive.

From our birth to our death God's "Light" lights our path and can keep us from going astray.

God's "Light" is as a lighthouse set upon a rocky crag, its light shinning for the whole world to see.

It never goes out even though the storm clouds of sin try to hide it from view.

It has guided many a soul to where it belongs, under the protection of God's almighty hand.

When sin tries to lead us astray, turn to God and His "Light" will comfort us and guide us home again.

God's "Light" cleanses the mind and the soul and controls what comes forth from our lips.

It guides our hand to reach out to those in need and restore their confidence in God.

God's "Light" will be the light of the new world to come, for the sun by day and the moon by night there will be no more need.

God's "Light" will shine in the lives of those who seek to do His will and brings all who love Him unto Himself.

God's "Light" was, is and always will be a guide to all who follow the straight and narrow path that leads to eternal life where there will be no more sin, disease, or death.

MOTHER

Luke 1:28

*A*n having come in, the angel said to her, "Rejoice, highly favored one, the Lord is with you, blessed are you among women."

M— Motherhood; a gift from God to women.

O— Organizer; the one who keeps the household running smoothly, cares for her family in a Christian way.

T— Tried and true; always there when needed, the last to complain, stands by her mate through thick and thin.

H— Helpmate; encourages her mate in his endeavor to supply his families needs, his lover and confidant.

E— Educator; sets the standards for her family, encourages them to follow Biblical ways.

R— Reliable; always dependable, never fails to assist when the family or church has needs.

By His Love

Deuteronomy 6:5

*Y*ou shall love the Lord your God with all your heart, with all your soul, with all your strength.

The love of Jesus Christ is deep within my soul and there it will unfold. It will reflect in the attitude I display towards my friends and family.

Like the child of God I am I cannot hold a grudge or seek revenge against those who have wronged me. It wasn't always so, for once I indulged in the sweetness of sin and never regarded Jesus anyone but someone who did not want me to have any fun.

Then came the day that my sinful ways found me out and in my hurting hour I turned to Jesus and through His love for me, He changed me from within.

Jesus saved me from a tragic death, death from the sins I was indulging in and for this I owe Him and I will praise Him and obey Him the rest of my life.

Sin still abounds, but now I have my Savior to guide my ship of life, with Him at the helm I am safe and assured of eternal life.

Jesus loves me beyond my comprehension, this I know because I asked Him to come and live in my heart and be my comforter.

Jesus died for my sins on the cross at Calvary, so now I walk the straight and narrow path that leads to eternal life.

Though Satan may tempt me to stray and offer me riches of silver and gold, I have my Savior to call upon to protect me and guide me through the temptations of this life.

I know in my heart that one day I will dwell in the house of my Lord when from this world he calls me, and then I will travel through the heavens above until I reach my eternal home.

So it will be with all who forsake their sinful ways and submit to the will of God and follow Him while on this earth they abide.

By Our Masters Hand

Revelation 22:1-2

And he showed me a pure river of water of life, clear as crystal, proceeding from the throne of God and of the Lamb. In the middle of its street, and on either side of the river, was the tree of life, which bore twelve fruits, each tree yielding its fruit every month. The leaves of the tree were for the healing of the nations.

In the heaves above, Jesus has prepared a place for the tried and true. Beyond our vision, there are streets of gold and walls of precious stone, put in place by our Master's hand.

A river of crystal-clear water flows from our Creator's throne, its water's will quench the souls of the followers of Jesus and there will be peace forevermore.

The fruit of the tree of life will be abundant and tasty too, no more seeds of sin or despair, for Jesus will be there.

Fields of flowers never seen before, they will be pleasing to the sight, colors never before seen by eyes like yours and mine, they will reflect the "Light" and love of our heavenly host.

The place we call heaven may be beyond the sky so high, but through the love of Jesus Christ it can your home and mine.

Old friends and new will greet us by the score, it will be as if we never left our heavenly home, our earthly ties will be no more, nor will the heartache and pain be remembered anymore.

Yes, there is a place far beyond the sky so blue, a place where there is peace and harmony too. The best news of all, our Master created it by His mighty hand just for you and me.

Pack your bags my friends, pack them with your heavenly deeds while on Earth you abode. You will leave all of your sins behind, for in heaven there is only love and harmony.

Be ready at a moment's notice to leave your earthly home, for when our heavenly Father calls our name to heaven we will go.

Worthy

Isaiah 55:7

*L*et the wicked forsake his way, and the unrighteous man his thoughts; let him return to the Lord, and He will have mercy on him; and to our God, for He will abundantly pardon.

O Lord God we the unrighteous seek Thy forgiveness so that we might become worthy to stand before Thy throne in adoration, and praise Thy holy name.

May the day come when those who worship Thee be allowed to enter Thy kingdom where there will be no more clouds of sin to keep us from worshiping You.

Gracious God bless us all as we go about our lives. May Your word light the path that You would have us to trod.

Like sinners of the past, we too wish to be cleansed of our sins and come under the shelter of Your wings.

The sins of this world overshadow us as we walk in the darkness thereof, only through Your love can we overcome.

Through the knowledge of Thy Son, Jesus Christ, we can become rich in Thy ways and able to accomplish that which You would have us to do.

It is here in this world that we have the opportunity to grow spiritually so that at the end of our earthly existence we might be granted permission to join You in heaven.

Through prayer and supplication, we come before Thee and partition You to heal those in need according to Your will.

Without You O Lord, we have no chance of living beyond this life. We are as clay in Your hands, mold us into the vessel that You would have us to be.

These things we ask in the name of Thy Son, Jesus Christ. A-men

 INGERPRINTS ON THE CROSS

Revelation 21:4

And God will wipe away every tear from their eyes; there shall be no more death, nor sorrow, nor crying. There shall be no more pain, for the former things have passed away.

My fingerprints are all over the cross at Calvary that held my Savior as He died.

It was my sins that caused Jesus to be tried and crucified on the cross at Calvary.

God sent His only Son, Jesus Christ, to take my place on the cross so that I would not have to die for the sins that can keep me from His side.

As Jesus stood before Pilate He never said a word, He endured the humiliation and the pain of the scourging that was meant for me.

101

It was my hands that held the nails and my hands that delivered the blows that drove the nails through His feet and his hands.

Jesus Christ gave His life so that sinners like you and me would not have to suffer and die the death of a sinner on the cross at Calvary.

Even though my sins convicted Jesus that faithful day, Jesus wiped my fingerprints from that cross at Calvary and set me free.

Glory be to God for allowing Jesus Christ to take my place on the cross, setting me free from the sins that can keep me from His side.

I no longer have to carry the burden of convicting Jesus and nailing him to the cross.

Through Jesus' death, burial and resurrection He revealed the way that leads to heaven and He has invited you and me to join Him when this world we leave.

SHIP OF LIFE

Romans 10:9

That if you confess with your mouth the Lord Jesus and believe in your heart that God has raised Him from the dead, you will be saved.

Our ship of life has been tattered and torn by the storms of sin and has suffered great loss. Only through the love of our Lord and Master, Jesus Christ are we able to survive.

Seas breaking on the reefs of temptation fills the air with a mist that can cloud the mind and entice us to stray.

Above the breaking seas of sin can be seen the light of a distant lighthouse shinning through the darkness of sin, warning all to beware of the dangers ahead.

Just as the lighthouse warns of dangers ahead, so does it give comfort to our soul that someone cares, His name is Jesus.

Jesus came to earth to pay the price of your sins and mine and while here opened the door through which we all one day must pass; the door of death awaits one and all.

Those who know Jesus and obey Him hold no fear of the door of death, for on the other side we will find Jesus holding out His hand, welcoming us home.

This life is short indeed, leaving us no time to waste in our pursuit of the knowledge of God, knowledge that will lead us to the foot of the cross.

The cross being a place or repentance, a place to lay down our burdens at the feet of Jesus and receive forgiveness of our sins.

Sins that can tear holes in our ship of life, sins that can weigh us down and keep us from becoming a child of the most High.

Jesus is indeed the one and only Son of God, the one who loved use enough to pay the price of your sins and mine by allowing His blood to be shed on a Roman cross.

Jesus has the power to save our ship of life from the reefs of sin and lead us home, a home in heaven where no longer there will be any danger of being blown about by the winds of sin.

$\mathcal{W}$HO ARE WE

John 1:12

$\mathcal{B}$ut as many as receive Him, to them He gave the right to become children of God, to those who believe in His name.

Lest we forget, we are children of God; we are to conduct ourselves at all times and under all circumstances as such.

As tempting as the pleasures of the flesh are, if they do not conform to the word of God, stop, remember whom you are representing and act accordingly.

Remember that at all times we are representatives of Jesus Christ, You and I are to set the example for others to follow, never once did Jesus go against the word of God and neither should we.

Self-discipline enhances our ability to live a more Christ like life, make the endeavor each day to put Jesus first in all of your decisions and actions, thus we will be better equipped to overcome the temptations of the world.

Jesus lived here on earth for a few short years and yet His influence is just as strong today in the lives of believers as it was over two thousand years ago.

God came to earth in the form of man through His Son Jesus Christ, Jesus came to earth on your behalf and mine, then as now Jesus reigns supreme over all things, great and small.

Jesus came to earth as a sacrifice for your sins and mine; He came to prove that sin is powerless against the word of God. He gave us permission to call upon and use His name whenever we find ourselves confronted by the temptations of Satan.

Lest we forget, Jesus shed His blood on the cross at Calvary and through this act set us free from the bondage of sin, thus enabling us to come before His throne and be cleansed from all unrighteousness.

Through our act of submission, we acknowledge that we are a child of God and as such, we hold no fear against the Day of Judgment. Jesus told us, "I am the way, the truth, and the life. All that believeth in Me shall not perish but have eternal life." Go forth as children of God and proclaim His word to all you meet.

$\mathscr{J}$esus Is The Reason For The Christmas Season

Matthew 1:18, 21

 ow the birth of Jesus Christ was as follows: After His mother Mary was betrothed to Joseph, before they came together, she was found with child of the Holy Spirit. 21; And she will bring forth a Son and you shall call His name Jesus, for he will save His people from their sins.

On a cold winter's night long ago our Lord and Savior was born in a manger; for there was no room in the Inn.

God came to earth and clothed Himself in human flesh and was called Jesus, the one and only Son of God is He.

O, what a noble deed, to leave the comfort of his heavenly home and come to earth to set mankind free from the bondage of sin and open the door to heaven.

His "Light" so shines before the whole world that many have left their sinful ways and have followed Him, O what a Savior is He.

Never seeking his own will, but the will of his Father who sent Him, submissive was He to the calling that lead Him to Calvary.

Jesus is your Lord and my Lord, never will we need anyone else to follow, His ways are straight and His teachings are true, follow Him and be blessed the rest of your days.

Jesus, the Son of God is of the trinity and has opened the scriptures so that all might come to know the truth, the truth that can set us free.

Come to know Jesus, come to know the one who holds our future in His hands; His love is extended to all, not just a select few.

As Christmas seasons comes and go remember that it was Jesus who came to earth those many years ago and made available the greatest gift of all, life eternal to all who accept Him as Lord and Savior.

Praise him young and old, praise Him for Jesus is the reason for the Christmas season, born of a virgin was He, love and obey Him is all that he asks of you and me.

$\mathcal{O}$UR JESUS

2 Corinthians 5:14-15

$\mathcal{F}$or the love of Christ compels us, because we judge thus, that if One died for all, then all died; and He died for all, that those who live should live no longer for themselves, but for Him who died for them and rose again.

Jesus loves us all; He gave His life on the cross of Calvary as a sacrifice for our sins. Through His sacrifice on the cross, He gave us life unto eternal life.

If we go astray and fall prey to sin, He will forgive us if we repent and turn from our sinful ways. Seventy times seventy He will forgive us, but if we die in our sins, He will cast us into outer darkness for all eternity.

Yes, Jesus loves us and if we will allow Him He will guide our feet on the path He wants us to trod. Jesus gave us freedom of choice, free to live our lives the way that we want to live or to follow Him. Either way we choose to live, He will honor our decision and love us regardless of our decission.

Jesus loves the beggar on the street just as much as He loves the wealthiest person in the world, He discriminates not, nor does He hold one dearer than the other. This may seem foreign to those who do not understand, His love is for all.

From the very beginning of the world, Jesus knew when and where each and everyone would be born and how we would live our lives. He set the standard for life and then backed away and allowed us to choose how we would live.

Those who choose to live life their way and ignore Jesus' calling will live to regret their decision, for on the Day of Judgment all shall account for how they lived their life while here on earth and receive their reward accordingly.

Through the scriptures we are encouraged to follow the ways of Jesus and allow Him to guide us through this life, in so doing we can avoid many of the pitfalls that await those who choose to live life their way.

There are only two forces in this world; the forces of good and the forces of evil. The forces of good come from and through Jesus, while the forces of evil comes from and are orchestrated by Satan. The two are not compatible; we either follow one or the other. We ourselves make that choice as to whom we want to follow Jesus or Satan. All are responsible for their own choice and will reap accordingly.

LD RUGGED CROSS

Matthew 10:38, 40

*A*nd he who does not take his cross and follow after Me is not worthy of Me. He who receives you receives Me, and he who receives Me receives Him who sent Me.

On a hill far away I stood one day before an Old Rugged Cross, one like the one upon which my Lord and Master gave His life so that you and I might be free.

I recall that just before darkness fell they removed His body and placed it in a tomb. Behold, in three days He triumphed over the grave.

Every time I watch a setting sun, it brings back the sorrow and pain I felt the day that they crucified my Lord. I can still see Him wince from the pain of those nails as they pierced His hands and feet.

Tears still flow when I see a Roman cross on a far away hill, it brings back memories of the day that Jesus shed His blood and washed me white as snow.

My Lord bore my sins that day and heavy were they. I heard him say, "My child, I did this just for you. Go, tell all who will hear that I will return to my Father's side and come again one day soon."

With these thoughts in mind I returned to my home, there I fell to my knees and prayed, "Dear Lord Jesus, thank You for taking my place on the Old Rugged Cross, for I of myself could not bear all of that sorrow and pain."

Every time I hear a hammer strike a nail my thoughts go back to the day that they nailed my Lord to the Old Rugged Cross, never again will I be the same.

That was the day that my Lord set me free from the bondage of sin and I came to see that sin is of the evil one, the one who wants to keep me from enjoying the love and freedom that my Lord Jesus wants for me.

When this world I leave I know that I will join my Lord in heaven and live with Him for eternity, free from the sins that now bind me to my cross, a cross that for now I must bear.

In that day I will join with the heavenly hosts and sing praises unto His Holy Name. There, I will bow before His throne and celebrate His victory over the Old Rugged Cross, a victory that He has passed on to me.

LAST REQUEST

John 15:23

*J*esus answered and said to him, "If anyone loves Me, he will keep my word; and My Father will love him, and We will come to him and make Our home with him.

Lord Jesus, creator of my earthly home, bless my family and friends, reach out and comfort them as my life here on earth comes to an end.

Console their souls as this life I prepare to leave behind and venture to my new home, one prepared for me from the beginning of time.

Time is short; I must go, for my Lord, Jesus Christ stands on yonder hill, the last hill I have to climb.

I am ready to leave, leave my earthly family and friends behind. Cry not for me, but rather pray for my safe journey home.

My life has been long and sometimes filled with woe, now all of that is behind me and I am ready to go home.

God gave me a full life with family and friends; I have no regrets about laying my life down and moving on to meet family and old friends who are waiting for me on the other side.

From my childhood till now my Lord and Savior, Jesus Christ, has blessed me and seen me through many hard times.

I have not walked this pathway of life alone, Jesus has walked it with me every step of the way and has consoled me when things went wrong and I could not see my way.

Through His comfort and love I have journeyed many a hard mile, never quite knowing how I would get there, but Jesus would take me by my hand as He is doing now, leading me home.

Comfort my family and friends Lord, let them know that it is all right for me to leave them and go home. My body is tired and my soul is ready to meet Jesus, there I will thank Jesus for coming to earth and setting me free from my sins.

My last request Lord Jesus is that You care for my friends and family as you have cared for me, light their path and guide them as Your "Light" has guided me.